Presented to

_____

By

_____

Date

_____

Doubt No More

A Simple Guide to Hearing God Answer Prayer

Mary Jo Sherwood

BTW PRESS

Minneapolis

Copyright © 2005 Mary Jo Sherwood

Published by BTW Press, LLC
Minneapolis, Minnesota

Unless otherwise indicated, the Scripture quotations contained herein are from the New Revised Standard Version Bible: Catholic Edition copyright© 1993 and 1989 by the Division of Christian Education of the National Council of the Churches of Christ in the U.S.A. Used by permission. All rights reserved.

Scripture quotations noted NIV are taken from the HOLY BIBLE, NEW INTERNATIONAL VERSION®, Copyright© 1973, 1978, 1984 by International Bible Society. Used by permission of Zondervan Publishing House. All rights reserved.

Scripture quotations marked (NLT) are taken from the Holy Bible, New Living Translation, copyright © 1996. Used by permission of Tyndale House Publishers, Inc., Wheaton, Illinois 60189. All rights reserved.

Cover design and graphics: Matt Moxness
Developmental Editing: Betty Liedtke
Copyediting: Connie Anderson / Peter Mohs
Proofreading: Emily Selenski
Author Photo: Sean O'Malley
Text Design/Layout: Caron Olhoft
Print Production: Reflections®

First Edition 2005

ISBN 0-9768039-0-9

Library of Congress Control Number 2005902946

Printed in the United States of America

To my husband, Frank

and to our children,

Ryan, Rachel, and Nathan

Contents

Introduction

All too often I hear people say, "I pray, but God never answers my prayers." Other people I encounter tell me that prayer is not a regular part of their day, their week or even their year. After all, why take the time to pray when they are not even sure that God will answer?

The Bible tells us that God does answer prayers. In the book, *Prayer of Jabez*, author Bruce Wilkinson gives an example of a single Biblical verse about God answering prayer, and he shows what a profound effect that verse had on him and others.

After I read the book, however, it occurred to me that surely there must be more than a single verse in the Bible that speaks about situations where God answers prayers. I started looking and found hundreds!

That revelation is what led to the book you are now reading. Though there have been times in my life when I had doubts as to whether God was answering my prayers, I can't imagine not praying. And in the time I've spent working on this book, God has continued answering my prayers in amazing and wonderful ways. Sometimes, God gives me the answers before I even ask the questions!

I hope this book will help you see that God does indeed answer our prayers, and that it will show you ways to establish and strengthen your own prayer life.

May God's blessings be upon you every moment of every day!

Mary Jo Sherwood

1

Knock, Knock

Here I am! I stand at the door and knock.
If anyone hears my voice and opens the door,
I will come in and eat with him, and he with me.

Revelations 3:20 NIV

L ife is overflowing with things to do, places to go, and people to see. It's no surprise that finding time to pray — let alone listening for an answer to our prayers — can be a challenge. Today people are running in multiple directions and rarely have time to sit down together for dinner, much less saying grace before a meal. The closest some people get to prayer is watching a *Hail Mary* pass during a football game. Even children are affected by the pace of our lives. God help us should we ever lose our day planners!

Simple logic dictates that 100 percent of the prayers we don't pray won't be answered. The poem, "The Difference," illustrates the need to take time to pray.

The Difference
I got up early one morning and rushed
right into the day;
I had so much to accomplish that
I didn't have time to pray.
Problems just tumbled about me,
and heavier came each task.
"Why doesn't God help me?"

He answered, "You didn't ask."
I tried to come into God's presence;
I used all my keys in the lock.
God gently and lovingly chided,
"My child, you didn't knock."
I woke up early this morning,
and paused before entering the day;
I had so much to accomplish
that I had to take time to pray.

Anonymous

Not only have we allowed ourselves to become overwhelmed and overscheduled, we've also become a society of instant gratification. When we ask for something, we want it NOW! When we make requests and decisions, we expect immediate answers and results. This is true even in our prayer life. If we ask God for something, we want an answer, and we expect to hear it immediately!

Many people also pray for one particular answer or outcome. They already know the one they want. If the answer God gives them isn't what they are expecting or hoping for, they close their minds and hearts and continue looking for the answer they want.

> A man lost his footing while hiking
> one day, and fell off the edge of a cliff.
> While tumbling down, he caught
> hold of a small branch.
> "HELP! IS ANYBODY UP THERE?"
> the climber shouted.
> A majestic voice boomed through the
> gorge: "I will help you, my child,
> but first you must have faith in me."
> "Yes, yes, I trust you!" cried the climber.
> "Let go of the branch," boomed the voice.
> There was a long pause, and the
> climber shouted up again,
> "IS THERE ANYONE ELSE UP
> THERE I COULD TALK TO?"
>
> Author Unknown

Like the climber, we too, are often unwilling to let go. We want to be in control of our own destiny, and we ask for what seems to us to be the best answer. Because we have limited insight and vision, we can't always see the bigger picture. What seems right and good for us today may not be so in the future. God, on the other hand, sees the whole picture. He knows what's best for us now and through eternity, and He answers our prayers accordingly. God gives us what we need when we need it, not what we think we want when we want it.

In Jeremiah 29:11, God tells us He has great plans for us. It is through prayer that we come to know and understand His plans for our lives. God is knocking at the door — ready, willing, and able to answer our prayers. The question is not whether God answers prayer, but whether we are willing to open the door to hear the answer.

Points to Ponder

1. How often do you turn to God each day?

2. What changes can you make in your daily schedule to find more time for prayer?

3. How can you be more aware of God's presence in your life?

◆ ◆ ◆

Lord, open my eyes and ears to your presence at my door.

2

Expect the Unexpected

Before they call I will answer,
while they are yet speaking I will hear.

Isaiah 65:24

If you were to close your eyes at this very moment, what would you hear? Other people talking, perhaps, or music playing. You might hear phones ringing, babies crying, horns honking, or sirens blaring. Our world is full of noise and distractions, but if we are going to hear God answering our prayers, we need to tune out all that is going on around us to be open to His presence. God says to us in Psalm 46:10: "Stop, be still and know that I am God." If we don't stop to sift through the noise and distractions, it is easy for us to miss the messages that God provides.

God utilizes a variety of options to speak to us to get His message across. While He may speak directly to one person, He could use an external source to speak to another. This could be a friend, a neighbor, or a total stranger. It could also be something we read in the newspaper or hear on TV. God communicates through Scripture, nature, people, events, the media, and what we often refer to as Divine Inspiration.

When we pray, God offers us options that will lead us to the best possible outcome. But we can't arrive at that outcome if we are not listening for God's message. The answer may be right in front of us, but we are not aware of it. We may see the answer, but not understand it, or we miss the answer entirely because we already know the answer we want and expect, and that is all we are looking for. We think we have it all figured out, and we expect God to hand it over exactly in accordance with our plans and agendas. Want to make God laugh? Tell Him your plans.

When I was in high school I studied Spanish, and after a year of learning the language I had the opportunity to travel to Mexico City. At one point, I found myself needing to ask for directions, so I bravely approached a local resident and asked — in Spanish — for directions. Although I listened carefully to his response, I was unable to comprehend what he was saying. I chalked it up to my limited knowledge of Spanish and my lack of familiarity with the words he used. I turned to my friend, who spoke fluent Spanish, and asked her to translate. She was surprised and amused at my request, since the person had answered me in English. I had expected to hear the response in Spanish, and since I wasn't listening for any other possibility, I wasn't able to understand an answer that had been given in my own language.

When we open our minds to all the possibilities before us, we see and hear with greater clarity. God does not overcomplicate things. However, He may speak to us and guide us in a way that we are not ready to understand, making it difficult for us to hear and follow directions.

A furious storm was raging, and it had been raining for days with no end in sight. As the floodwaters continued to rise, a very pious man stood praying for God to rescue him.

A little while later, someone came by in a car and said, "Let me take you to higher ground."

The man replied, "No, God will save me."

The waters grew higher and someone in a boat rowed by saying, "Come quickly into my boat."

The man replied, "No thank you. God

will save me." Finally the waters rose up to the roof. The man scrambled up to the highest spot.

A helicopter flew overhead, and a voice from inside yelled out, "Climb aboard."

"No, God will save me," the man yelled back.

The waters continued to rise and alas, the man drowned. He went to heaven and poured out his heart before God.

"I was always pious, I prayed to You everyday, and still You let me drown. Why did You not answer my prayers?" he asked.

God answered, "Who do you think sent the car, the boat, and the helicopter?"

Author Unknown

By expecting God to answer our prayers in a certain way, we often miss the message. This causes us difficulty in seeing God at work in our lives even when it should be obvious. Perhaps we should be more like children, who hear God answer because they have no preconceived notion of how He will answer, or what answer He will give. Children don't analyze answers like adults; they simply accept them. When we are subconsciously seeking to hear the answer we expect, rather than God's answer, we are praying not that His will be done, but that He approve of ours.

Listening is the beginning of prayer.

Mother Teresa

Points to Ponder

1. What can you do to eliminate distractions while you are praying?

2. When praying, do you allow God time to answer, and are you open to answers other than the one you want or expect?

3. Think of any recent prayers that God may have answered, even if initially it didn't seem as though He did. What means did God use to answer?

◆ ◆ ◆

Lord, open my mind to the possibilities that you place before me.

3

Pick Me!

*"Lord, do you not care that my sister has left me to do all the work by myself? Tell her then to help me."
But the Lord answered her, "Martha, Martha, you are worried and distracted by many things; there is need of only one thing. Mary has chosen the better part, which will not be taken away from her."*

Luke 10:40-42

Doesn't it feel great to be chosen? Chosen for the baseball team, for the school play or for the dream job that provides us with big bucks, lots of prestige, and a corner office to boot! We all enjoy being chosen, but how many of us strive to be chosen by God?

John 3:16 tells us: "God so loved the world that He gave us His only Son. . . ." God's unending love for each of us calls us in a unique way to create a relationship with Him. Our willingness to develop that relationship directly impacts our ability to hear God answer our prayers.

Prayer itself allows us to have a conversation with God. It fulfills a desire to talk to Him and tell Him what's going on in our lives. Simply saying a prayer, however, is not the same thing as having a relationship with God. A relationship is based on two-way conversations. It involves sharing all aspects of our lives: the joys, the sorrows, the questions, and the advice. If we talk to God through prayer but don't listen for His response, we have not yet developed a relationship with Him; we have not made Him an active part of our lives.

The level of communication that people have with each other depends on the level of trust between them. Casual acquaintances can talk comfortably and endlessly with each other about the weather, sports, or current events. To develop a real relationship, however, they must get to know each other. Developing enough trust and confidence to open their hearts to each other requires communication from both. It can't be a one-way street.

It takes both talking and listening to build the trust that leads to the development of deeper relationships. The same is true of our relationship with God. Choosing to have conversations with God through prayer will lead to deeper levels of communication. It is not just saying a prayer that gets results, but rather it is spending time talking and listening to God that brings us answers.

A wise person once told me that a true friend is someone with whom you can pick up right where you left off, no matter how long it's been since you've seen or spoken with each other. Even after years, when one of you picks up the phone and calls the other, it seems as though you just saw each other the day before. It's like that with God. No matter how long it's been since your last conversation, you can pick up right where you left off. God will never turn His back on you.

God has chosen each of us, and He is waiting for us to respond to His invitation to enter into a deeper relationship with Him. Just as Mary and Martha were given the opportunity to spend time developing a relationship with Christ, we, too, have the opportunity to make the same choice that Mary made. It is up to us whether we choose to use prayer to include God as an active part of our lives. God says, "Pick me!" so that you can enjoy all the blessings that He has waiting for you.

Points to Ponder

1. Thinking back to a time when you were selected for a team, an honor, or an award, Can you relate this to the joy of being chosen by God?

2. What is the most joyful, and the most sorrowful, experience you have brought to God in prayer?

3. What steps can you take that will help you enter into a deeper relationship with God?

◆ ◆ ◆

Lord, open my heart that I may enter into a deeper relationship with You.

4

In God We Trust

Trust in the LORD with all your heart;
do not depend on your own understanding.
Seek His will in all you do, and He will direct your paths.

Proverbs 3:5-6 NLT

The cornerstone for developing a strong relation-ship with God is trust. Through the process of prayer we come to realize, as we do in other areas of our lives, that we do not need to rely solely on our own understanding. Just as we put our trust in our pediatrician when we are the parents of a newborn, or we turn to financial advisors and business consultants to guide us in managing our money or running a cor-poration, prayer allows us to consult with God and helps us to trust God to show us the way.

> Mother Teresa reminds us that,
> "God does not call the equipped,
> He equips the called."

Even though we do not know exactly how God's plan will unfold, we are called to respond "Yes." Mary is a perfect example of someone who did. She accepted the call to be the mother of Jesus, trusting that God would guide her. Mary became the first — and ultimate — example of discipleship. Without her dependence and obedience, there would be no Bethlehem story. Through her complete faith and surrender to God, she modeled for us what it means to say, "Yes."

It was in prayer that Mary allowed the strength and power of God to become real in her life. At the wedding at Cana, her understanding of God's power led her to intercede on behalf of others. When she said four seemingly insignificant words to Jesus, "They have no wine," she was really saying, "Jesus, they need your help." She already knew without a doubt that He was the one who could assist them in their hour of need. And when Jesus responded to her request, she immediately turned to the others and said: "Do as He says." With these words, she instructed them to trust Him.

That trust is an essential element in hearing and accepting God's answer to our prayers — trust that God won't let us down. Actress Marlene Dietrich once said that true friends are the ones you can call at 4 a.m. But even our most trusted friends cannot always be there when we need them. As much as these friends would like to support us, life sometimes gets in the way of their ability to do so.

Only God has the power to ALWAYS be there for us. With God, nothing is impossible. And in the end, only God can sustain us when all else fails.

Even so, "always" is a difficult concept to embrace. We want to believe that God answers each and every request, but at times we still have doubts. The devil's greatest ally is that doubt, which causes us to question whether God has the integrity and ability to stand behind His promises. The difficulty lies in our ability to truly believe that God could possibly care that much about us.

If anybody should have had clarity that God can and does answer prayers, it was Peter. As a disciple and friend, Peter saw Jesus perform many miracles firsthand. Still, Peter experienced doubt. Peter knew Jesus personally. Even so, his faith wavered at times. He had just witnessed the miracle of the loaves and the fishes when Jesus appeared on the water in the middle of a storm. Jesus called Peter to come out onto the water, and Peter stepped out of the boat in faith.

However, he started to sink when he lost focus and stopped placing his trust in God.

When we keep our focus on God, it is easy to trust Him. But when we let outside or unknown forces distract us, as Peter did with his fear of the storm, that's when we will have doubts. That's when we can start to sink.

As Peter came to know, a personal relationship with God through prayer is more than just asking for what we want or what we need, it is placing our trust in God and accepting the answers that we are given. God releases the grace to help us understand those answers. When we place our trust in Him, He provides us with new insights and direction, and gives us the strength and perseverance to move forward, trusting that He will direct us every step of the way.

Points to Ponder

1. What are some areas of your life where you have difficulty trusting God?

2. Where do you most feel that God's presence is missing in your life?

3. What can you do to place more trust in God, and to put control in God's hands, instead of your own?

◆ ◆ ◆

Lord, help me to trust in You. Help me to let go of my need to be in control, so that I may turn control of my life over to You through prayer.

5

A Helping Hand

*We know that all things work together
for good for those who love God,
who are called according to his purpose.*

Romans 8:28

Prayer helps us to know the will of God for our lives, and to know that we can rely on His knowledge and wisdom to guide the decisions we make. More than just asking God for what we want, prayer helps us to welcome and accept all that occurs in our lives. Scripture tells us that God knows every hair on our head and every beat of our heart, and that He will provide what we need.

Still, many people find it difficult to ask for God's help and guidance, even in times of crisis. It is just too hard to give up control and to rely on someone else, even God! That's why it's common for us to pray about a situation in our lives while still trying to control the outcome ourselves. And when that outcome doesn't occur, we assume that God is not answering our prayer. Actually, the opposite is true. God always answers. But we have to let go of the desired answer we are holding on to in order to hear and accept God's answer. Sometimes that answer is "yes," sometime it's "no," and sometimes it's "wait."

It takes courage, strength, and faith to let go of our need to be in control and get past the "I can do it on my own" attitude and ask for help. If we are going to succeed at anything in life, that is exactly what we need to do. When we rely too much on ourselves and too little on God, we fail to hear God answer our prayers. By trusting that God will lead us in the right direction — knowing what's best for us and providing for our needs — we move the focus from ourselves to God.

Unfortunately, trusting and depending on others is not always easy or comfortable. We are taught from an early age that to succeed in life we must learn to be independent and self-sufficient. We must accomplish things on our own. Dependence on other people is seen as weak or unwise. After all, "if you want something done right, you have to do it yourself."

Most of us can probably recall an experience, either at our job or in school, when a group project fell apart because one or more people in the group did not complete their share of the work. Perhaps we had to pick up the slack so that our own job or grade would not be jeopardized, or maybe we ended up looking bad even though our own work was done well. Either way, this type of experience leaves us believing that we cannot depend on other people, or that we need a contingency plan just in case others do not do their part.

On the other hand, isn't it wonderful when we don't have to worry about somebody else holding up their end of the bargain? When we know that that person will not only do the work they promised to do, but we can count on them to take over part of our load if it gets too heavy or overwhelming.

There is someone like that. Someone who knows and cares about us, who understands our problems, and who has our best interests at heart. That someone is God. He is always there, always faithful, always doing His part. He helps us handle the challenges we face and He reassures us that He loves us unconditionally. Through prayer we come to realize that it's okay to depend on God instead of ourselves. In fact, it's not just okay — it's essential!

Socrates once said: "Our prayers should be for blessings in general, for God knows what is good for us." When we pray in this manner, we are working hand in hand with God, fulfilling the life He has planned for us. While we may not understand His answers, by accepting them we are shifting the responsibility of the outcome to God, where it belongs.

As we grow in our relationship with God, we begin to understand God's love and His concern for us. Prayer allows each of us to discern our unique gifts and to become the person God calls us to be. We should never be afraid to ask God for help — either for ourselves or for others. And we should never be afraid to use the gifts that God has given us. That's what they are for.

> "When I stand before God at the end
> of my life, I would hope that I would
> not have a single bit of talent left,
> and could say, 'I used everything
> you gave me.'"
>
> Erma Bombeck

These inspiring words encourage us to live according to God's purpose and to use His gifts for the greater good. Thus prayer provides us with the opportunity and responsibility of helping others. We are called to pray for other people, not because God doesn't know their needs, or because He requires a certain number of prayers before He will act, but because God invites us to work with Him, sharing our gifts and growing in our own faith while serving others.

Through prayer we become, in the words of the Prayer of St. Francis, "channels of peace," receiving help from God for ourselves and becoming God's helping hands through which His grace, mercy, and love can reach out to the rest of the world.

Prayer of St. Francis

Lord, make me an instrument of thy peace.
Where there is hatred, let me sow love.
Where there is injury, pardon.
Where there is doubt, faith.
Where there is despair, hope.
Where there is darkness, light.
Where there is sadness, joy.

Oh Divine Master, grant that
I may not so much seek
to be consoled as to console,
to be understood as to understand,
to be loved as to love.
For it is in giving that we receive,
it is in pardoning that we are pardoned,
and it is in dying that we are born to
eternal life.

Points to Ponder

1. In what circumstances do you ask God for help?

2. How might you use your prayer life to ask for help for yourself, or to offer help to others?

3. What unique gifts do you feel God has given to you, and how can you use them to be a conduit of God's love to others?

◆ ◆ ◆

Lord, help me to seek your assistance in all I do.

6

The Ah Ha! Factor

I will pray to you, Lord;
answer me, God, at a time You choose.

Psalm 69:13

Everything happens for a reason. That's a lesson I learned from my grandmother years ago, but even so I sometimes forget that trials and tribulations are often blessings in disguise. We all experience things that, from time to time, may seem negative to us no matter how we look at them, but God will reveal their blessings if we ask Him. We just need to be patient and open and wait for the insight to understand His answer.

Throughout his life, my son has struggled in school. At the start of each new school year, I have met with teachers and administrators, trying to educate the educators about my son's strengths and weaknesses in the classroom. During all this time my prayer to God was: "Help me understand how to help him." At a particularly low point in this process, while dealing with staff changes, incompatible personalities and teaching styles, and feelings of doubt and despair that left me wondering if I was strong enough to go through it all again, a chance statement led to a "light bulb" moment for one of the counselors. A new series of questions and answers led to the revelation that my son had a condition that was virtually unknown and rarely diagnosed when he first started school.

As these events unfolded, God once again answered my prayers. With His infinite wisdom, He showed me a new way to look at the situation. He revealed that this series of events was an integral stepping-stone toward learning to help my son find the way to work with the gifts God had given him.

In His answers, God's blessings are abundant. Oftentimes He reveals them to us slowly and gradually when we are able to accept and understand them. It's much the same as when a parent teaches a child. If the child asks where babies come from, the parent would explain it differently, depending on whether the child was a toddler, a six-year-old, or a thirteen-year-old.

Our relationship with God works in the same way. The more mature our relationship, the greater our capacity to understand God's purpose in our lives. This type of maturity, however, does not come with age but through building a personal relationship with

God. And that can occur at any age by simply turning our focus to God in prayer.

God reveals more to us each time we enter into a conversation with Him. Think of your relationship with your best friends. When you first met, all you knew about each other were your names. But with each new encounter, each new conversation, you learned more about them — where they lived, where they grew up, information about their families, stories about their past and challenges they were facing in the present.

If something bad were to happen to them, not only would you be concerned, but you would know instinctively what they needed and how to help them. Your relationship is similar to that of a married couple who can finish each other's sentences, or have an entire conversation without either one uttering a full sentence.

If we look at our life experiences from a different perspective, we will often find "ah ha" moments where we can start to see God reveal to us who He is and how He is working in our lives. Each time we pray is a new experience because we have different needs and concerns. With each answer, no matter what it is, we continue to gain new insights and perspectives. Just as our true friends will give us needed advice over and over again until we finally "get it," God too waits for us to get it.

These "ah ha" moments help to open our eyes to God's presence in our lives and His great love for us. We can be oblivious to all that happens as life unfolds, or we can be open to discover the moments that reveal God's answer to our prayers. The more we pray, the more we realize that what seem like coincidences are really *God*-cidences.

Some call it fate, others call it serendipity, but these are not simply coincidences. They are a part of God's greater plan. Our whole attitude can change to become one of gratitude, faithfulness, and acceptance when we come to understand that God will bring to pass whatever it is He has led us to pray for, even if it's not what we had in mind in the first place.

> The value of consistent prayer is
> not that He will hear us,
> but rather that we will hear Him.
>
> William McGill

Points to Ponder

1. What signs might God be providing to assure you that it is He who is answering your prayers?

2. What seemingly unimportant events have occurred that may actually be part of the answers you've been seeking?

3. Are there any experiences in which you've had an "ah ha" moment through prayer?

◆ ◆ ◆

Lord, help me to patiently wait for you
to reveal the answer to my prayers.

7

Beyond the Shadow of a Doubt

And this is the boldness we have in Him,
that if we ask anything according to His will, He hears us.
And if we know that He hears us in whatever we ask,
we know that we have obtained the requests made of Him.

I John 5:14-15

Through the very process of praying, our lives are changed. God initiates that process through His unending love and calls each of us in a unique way to create a relationship with Him. But relationships do not happen overnight; they require work and perseverance. Anything worth pursuing is worth the time it takes to do so.

Developing a prayer life is much like learning to play a musical instrument or ride a bike. It is a struggle until we get the hang of it and, even then, it takes time before we feel confident and comfortable. But once we do, a whole new world opens up to us.

It's the same with prayer. Learning how to do it is merely the first step. In order to enjoy long-lasting results, we have to keep it up on a regular and consistent basis until it becomes a habit. But when prayer becomes a regular part of our lives, we begin to see more results and benefits for ourselves and for others than we could have ever believed possible.

So what is the best way to pray? What are the

steps that will most quickly and effectively establish a strong and fulfilling relationship with God through prayer?

There is no "one-size-fits-all" method of praying, just as there is no "one-and-only" way to exercise. Whether you ride a bike, walk on a treadmill, lift weights at the gym, or jog through your neighborhood, you will experience the benefits of exercise.

You must do whatever feels right to you and motivates you to keep it up. You can read or recite traditional prayers or you can have an informal and impromptu conversation with God. You can meditate in quiet reflection or you can use a journal to express your thoughts and concerns by writing to, for, or about God.

Remember that prayer itself is a gift from God. Pray in the manner, the place, and the time that feels most comfortable and appropriate for you. The most important thing is not how or where you are praying, but rather that you are praying. Your goal should be to establish and maintain the prayer life that works best for you. Start by simply asking God to guide you. Once you do that, you've already begun. You've taken the first step in the most rewarding journey you can possibly imagine.

As you begin, it may help to talk to other people and find out what works best for them. However, remember that the goal is to establish and maintain a prayer life that works best for you. Here are a few suggestions to help you get started:

Steps to Prayer

1. Place yourself in God's presence. Create good habits — it's hard to talk to someone you don't know. Study your faith, open the Bible and get to know God.

2. Examine your conscience. Reflect on actions you have taken in your life, and the purposes you had in doing so.

3. Meditate and converse with God. Adopt an attitude of, "Speak Lord, your servant is listening," rather than, "Listen Lord, your servant is speaking." Listening and pondering will allow God to dwell in you.

4. Be open to change. You cannot walk with God and stay the same. Ask for the strength and courage to see, hear, and accept what God is saying, and make the changes necessary.

5. Always say "Thank you." The more you do, the more you will realize that prayer itself is a gift that fills us with the grace of God. Appreciate everything that God is doing in your life, no matter how challenging or insignificant it may seem.

Remember that prayer does not change God; it changes the hearts of those who pray. And when we open our hearts, we will know beyond the shadow of a doubt that God is truly answering our prayers.

Points to Ponder

1. What type of prayer is most comfortable for you?

2. Is there another method of prayer you would consider trying?

3. What steps will you take to make prayer a daily habit and to establish a consistent prayer life?

◆ ◆ ◆

Lord, teach me to pray at all times.

The Next Step ...

As for me, I will certainly not sin against the Lord by ending my prayers for you ... But be sure to fear the Lord and sincerely worship him. Think of all the wonderful things he has done for you.

1 Samuel 12: 23-24 NIV

How different would the world be if we all took time to pray on a regular basis — If we listened first so that we could really hear God answering our prayers?

It is not a coincidence that you chose to read this book — it is a *God*-cidence. Maybe you've been moved to make some changes in your prayer life, or maybe you've been inspired to share this book with a friend or relative. Whether this is your first encounter with prayer or you have been praying for years, this book can be a resource for nurturing your prayer life.

At times prayer might be difficult, but remember that everything worthwhile takes time and effort. No matter where you are in your prayer life, you will still have occasions of doubt. Fortunately, God tells us that we don't have to go it alone. The Scriptures that follow provide numerous examples in which someone asked and God answered.

These verses are by no means the only Scriptures that reference God answering prayers; they are designed to be a starting guide to help you get better acquainted with God and the prayers God indeed answers. When you most need an answer, when you have the greatest doubts, turn to the Scriptures here to give you hope and strength. For Scripture tells us time and time again that God truly does answer prayer.

Open your mind,

Open your heart,
and

God will open your eyes!

Mary Jo Sherwood

Scriptures
for
Reflection

*For everything that was written in the past was written
to teach us, so that through endurance and the encouragement
of the Scriptures we might have hope.*

Romans 15:4 NIV

FAITH

*Trust, belief, hope, reliance, confidence, assurance,
loyalty, conviction*

Truly I tell you, if you say to this mountain, "Be taken up and thrown into the sea," and if you do not doubt in your heart, but believe that what you say will come to pass, it will be done for you. So I tell you whatever you ask for in prayer, believe that you have received it, and it will be yours.

Mark 11:23-24

If any of you is lacking in wisdom, ask God, who gives to all generously and ungrudgingly, and it will be given you. But ask in faith, never doubting, for the doubter, being double-minded and unstable in every way, must not expect to receive anything from the Lord.

James 1:5-6, 8

If you abide in me, and my words abide in you, ask for whatever you wish and it will be done.

John 15:7

Jesus said to her, "Did I not tell you that if you believed, you would see the glory of God?" So they took away the stone. And Jesus looked upward and said, "Father, I thank you for having heard me. I know that you always hear me, but I have said this for the sake of the crowd standing here, so that they may believe that you sent me."

John 11:40-42

Jesus said to him, "What do you want me to do for you?" The blind man said to him, "My teacher, let me see again." Jesus said to him, "Go; your faith has made you well." Immediately he regained his sight and followed him on the way.

Mark 10:51-52

I call upon you for you will answer me, O God; incline your ear to hear my words.

Psalms 17:6

Then suddenly a woman who had been suffering from hemorrhages for twelve years came up behind him and touched the fringe of his cloak, for she said to herself, "If only I touch his cloak, I will be made well." Jesus turned, and seeing her he said, "Take heart, daughter; your faith has made you well." And instantly the woman was made well.

Matthew 9:20-22

The Lord said to Moses, "I will do the very thing that you have asked; for you have found favor in my sight, and I know you by name.

Exodus 33:17

For I know the plans I have for you, declares the Lord, plans to prosper you and not to harm you, plans to give you hope and a future. Then you will call upon me and come and pray to me, and I will listen to you. You will seek me and find me when you seek me with all your heart.

Jeremiah 29:11-13 NIV

Faith

REFLECTIONS

FORGIVENESS

Mercy, reconciliation, iniquity, compassion,
sympathy, release, pardon, absolution

Hear my cry, O Lord. Pay attention to my prayer. Lord, if you kept a record of our sins, who, O Lord, could ever survive? But you offer forgiveness, that we might learn to fear you. O Israel, hope in the LORD; for with the LORD there is unfailing love and an overflowing supply of salvation.

Psalms 130:1-4, 7 NLT

Then he said, "Jesus, remember me when you come into your kingdom." He replied, "Truly I tell you, today you will be with me in Paradise."

Luke 23:42-43

Many times he delivered them, but they were rebellious in their purposes, and were brought low through their iniquity. Nevertheless he regarded their distress when he heard their cry. For their sake he remembered his covenant, and showed compassion according to the abundance of his steadfast love.

Psalms 106:43-45

Whenever you stand praying, forgive, if you have anything against anyone; so that your Father in heaven may also forgive your trespasses.

Mark 11:25

If people who are called by my name humble themselves, pray, seek my face and turn from their wicked ways, then I will hear from heaven, and will forgive their sin and heal their land.

2 Chronicles 7:14

The prayer of the faithful will save the sick, and the Lord will raise them up; and anyone who has committed sins will be forgiven. Therefore confess your sins to one another, so that you may be healed. The prayer of the righteous is powerful and effective.

James 5:15-16

"Forgive the iniquity of this people according to the greatness of your steadfast love, just as you have pardoned this people, from Egypt even until now." Then the Lord said, "I do forgive, just as you have asked."

Numbers 14:19-20

Then I acknowledged my sin to you, and did not hide my iniquity; I said, "I will confess my transgressions to the Lord," and you forgave the guilt of my sin. Therefore let all who are faithful offer prayer to you.

Psalms 32:5-6

"The tax collector, standing far off, would not even look up to heaven, but was beating his breast and saying, 'God be merciful to me, a sinner!' I tell you this man went down to his home justified rather than the other; for all who exalt themselves will be humbled, but all who humble themselves will be exalted."

Luke 18:13-14

He said, "If now I have found favor in your sight, O Lord, I pray, the Lord go with us. Although this is a stiff-necked people, pardon our iniquity and our sin, and take us for your inheritance." God said: I hereby make a covenant; and all the people among whom you live shall see the work of the Lord.

Exodus 34:9-10

REFLECTIONS

INTERCESSION

Prayer for others, mediation, appeal,
intervention, restoration,

Again, truly I tell you, if two of you agree on earth about anything you ask, it will be done for you by my Father in heaven. For where two or three are gathered in my name, I am there among them.

Matthew 18:19-20

And the Lord restored the fortunes of Job when he prayed for his friends; and the Lord gave Job twice as much as he had before.

Job 42:10

Samuel cried out to the Lord for Israel, and the Lord answered him.

1 Samuel 7:9

Then Elisha prayed: "O Lord, please open his eyes that he may see." So the Lord opened the eyes of the servant, and he saw.

2 Kings 6:17

Likewise the Spirit helps us in our weakness; for we do not know how to pray as we ought, but that very Spirit intercedes with sighs too deep for words. And God, who searches the heart, knows what is the mind of the Spirit, because the Spirit intercedes for the saints according to the will of God.

Romans 8:26-27

Then he stretched himself upon the child three times, and cried out to the Lord, "O Lord my God, let this child's life come into him again." The Lord listened to the voice of Elijah; the life of the child came into him again, and he revived.

1 Kings 17:21-22

"Answer me, O Lord, answer me, so that this people may know you, O Lord, our God, and that you have turned their hearts back." Then the fire of the Lord fell and consumed the burnt offering . . . When all the people saw it, they fell on their faces and said, "The Lord indeed is God, the Lord indeed is God."

1 Kings 18:37-39

Brothers and sisters, pray for us, so that the word of the Lord may spread rapidly and be glorified everywhere, just as it is among you, and that we may be rescued from wicked and evil people; for not all have faith. But the Lord is faithful; he will strengthen you and guard you from the evil one.

2 Thessalonians 3:1-3

Pray in the Spirit at all times in every prayer and supplication. To that end keep alert and always persevere in supplication for all the saints. Pray also for me, so that when I speak, a message may be given to me to make known with boldness the mystery of the gospel.

Ephesians 6:18-19

Hezekiah prayed for them, saying, "The good Lord pardon all who set their hearts to seek God, the Lord, the God of their ancestors, even though not in accordance with the sanctuary's rules of cleanness." The Lord heard Hezekiah and healed the people.

2 Chronicles 30:18-20

REFLECTIONS

PETITION

*Prayer for oneself, plea, request,
supplication, implore*

Ask, and it will be given you; search, and you will find; knock, and the door will be opened for you. For everyone who asks receives, and for everyone who knocks, the door will be opened.

Matthew 7:7-8

Jabez called on the God of Israel, saying, "Oh that you would bless me indeed, and enlarge my territory, that your hand would be with me, and that you would keep me from evil, that I may not cause pain." So God granted him what he requested.

1 Chronicles 4:10

For this child I prayed; and the Lord has granted me the petition that I made to him.

1 Samuel 1: 27

Incline your ear, O Lord, and answer me, for I am poor and needy. Give ear, O Lord, to my prayer; listen to my cry of supplication. In the day of my trouble I call on you, for you will answer me.

Psalms 86:1, 6-7

I will do whatever you ask in my name, so that the Father may be glorified in the Son. If in my name you ask me for anything, I will do it.

John 14:13-14

Thus says the Lord, the God of your ancestor David: "I have heard your prayer, I have seen your tears, indeed I will heal you."

2 Kings 20:2-3, 5

In the days of his flesh, Jesus offered prayers and supplication, with loud cries and tears, to the one who was able to save him from death, and he was heard because of his reverent submission.

Hebrews 5:7

One of his disciples said to him, "Lord, teach us to pray, as John taught his disciples." He said to them, "When you pray, say: 'Father, hallowed be your name. Your kingdom come. Give us each day our daily bread. And forgive our sins, for we ourselves forgive everyone indebted to us. And do not bring us to the time of trial.'"

Luke 11:1-4

So we fasted and petitioned our God for this, and he listened to our entreaty.

Ezra 8:23

About midnight Paul and Silas were praying and singing hymns to God, and the prisoners were listening to them. Suddenly there was an earthquake, so violent that the foundations of the prison were shaken; and immediately all the doors were opened and everyone's chains were unfastened.

Acts 16:25-26

REFLECTIONS

PRAISE

Exalt, extol, glorify, adoration,
appreciation, worship

I will bless the Lord at all times; his praise shall continually be in my mouth. I sought the Lord, and he answered me, and delivered me from all my fears.

Psalms 34:1, 4

I pray that you may have the power to comprehend, with all the saints, what is the breadth and length and height and depth, and to know the love of Christ that surpasses knowledge, so that you may be filled with all the fullness of God. Now to him who by the power at work within us is able to accomplish abundantly far more than all we can ask or imagine, to him be glory in the church and in Christ Jesus to all generations, forever and ever. Amen.

Ephesians 3: 16-21

Praise is due to you, O God, in Zion, and to you shall vows be performed, O you who answer prayer!

Psalms 65:1-2

I will praise the name of God with a song; I will magnify him with thanksgiving. Let the oppressed see it and be glad; you who seek God, let your hearts revive. For the Lord hears the needy, and does not despise his own that are in bonds.

Psalms 69:30, 32-33

To you, O God of my ancestors, I give thanks and praise, for you have given me wisdom and power, and have now revealed to me what we asked of you.

Daniel 2:23

But truly God has listened; he has given heed to the words of my prayer. Blessed be God, because he has not rejected my prayer or removed his steadfast love from me.

Psalms 66:19-20

"With what shall I come before the Lord, and bow myself before God on high?" He had told you, O mortal, what is good; and what does the Lord require of you but to do justice, to love kindness, and to walk humbly with your God.

Micah 6:6, 8

I waited patiently for the Lord; he inclined to me and heard my cry. He drew me up from the desolate pit, out of the miry bog, and set my feet upon a rock, making my steps secure. He put a new song in my mouth, a song of praise to our God.

Psalms 40:1-3

I will continue to rejoice, for I know that through your prayers and the help of the Spirit of Jesus Christ this will turn out for my deliverance.

Philippians 1:19

Make joyful noise to God, all the earth; sing the glory of his name; give to him glorious praise. Say to God, "How awesome are your deeds!" Come and see what God has done; he is awesome in his deeds among mortals.

Psalms 66:1-3, 5

REFLECTIONS

PROTECTION

Refuge, fortress, shelter, sheild, defense, safety,
guard, deliverance

One thing I ask of the Lord; this is what I seek: that I may dwell in the house of the Lord all the days of my life, to gaze on the beauty of the Lord and to seek him in his temple. For in the day of trouble he will keep me safe in his dwelling; He will hide me in the shelter of his tabernacle and set me high upon a rock.

Psalms 27:4-5 NIV

Then Jonah prayed to the Lord his God from the belly of the fish, saying, "I call to the Lord out of my distress, and he answered me." Then the Lord spoke to the fish, and it spewed Jonah out upon the dry land.

Jonah 2:1-2, 10

In distress you called, and I rescued you; I answered you in the secret place of thunder.

Psalms 81:7

Then they cried to the Lord in their trouble, and he saved them from their distress; He sent out his word and healed them, and delivered them from destruction.

Psalms 107:19-20

Protect me, O God, for in you I take refuge. I say to the Lord, "You are my Lord; I have no good apart from you." You show me the path of life. In your presence there is fullness of joy; in your right hand are pleasures forever more.

Psalms 16:1-2, 11

Those who love me, I will deliver; I will protect those who know my name. When they call to me, I will answer them; I will be with them in trouble, I will rescue them and honor them. With long life will satisfy them, and show them my salvation.

Psalms 91:14-16

It will be a sign and a witness to the Lord of hosts in the land of Egypt; when they cry to the Lord because of oppressors, He will send them a savior, and will defend and deliver them.

Isaiah 19:20

Away from me, all you who do evil, for the Lord has heard my weeping. The Lord has heard my cry for mercy; the Lord accepts my prayer. All my enemies will be ashamed and dismayed; they will turn back in sudden disgrace.

Psalms 6:8-10 NIV

Evening and morning and at noon I utter my complaint and moan, and he will hear my voice. He will redeem me unharmed from the battle that I wage, for many are arrayed against me.

Psalms 55:17-18

Hear my prayer O Lord; let my cry come to you. Do not hide your face from me in the day of distress. Incline your ear to me; answer me speedily the day I call.

Psalms 102:1-2

REFLECTIONS

STRENGTH

Fortitude, vigor, talent, capability,
courage, power, skill

Three times I appealed to the Lord about this, that it would leave me, but he said to me, "My grace is sufficient for you, for power is made perfect in weakness." So, I will boast all the more gladly of my weakness, so that the power of Christ may dwell in me. Therefore I am content with weaknesses, insults, hardships, persecutions, and calamities for the sake of Christ; for whenever I am weak, then I am strong.

2 Corinthians 12:8-10

Then you shall call, and the Lord will answer; you shall cry for help, and he will say, "Here I am." The Lord will guide you continually, and satisfy your needs in parched places.

Isaiah 58:9-11

When the righteous cry for help, the Lord hears, and rescues them from all their troubles.

Psalms 34:17

O Lord, you will hear the desire of the meek; you will strengthen their hearts; you will incline your ear to do justice for the orphan and the oppressed so that no one on earth may strike terror again.

Psalms 10:17-18

If disaster comes upon us, the sword, judgment, or pestilence, or famine, we will stand before this house, and before you, for your name is in this house, and cry to you in our distress, and you will hear and save.

2 Chronicles 20:9

I called upon your name, O Lord, from the depths of the pit; you heard my plea, "Do not close your ear to my cry for help, but give me relief!" You came near when I called on you; you said, "Do not fear!" You have taken up my cause, O Lord, you have redeemed my life.

Lamentations 3:55-58

The Lord is my rock, my fortress, and my deliverer. I call upon the Lord, who is worthy to be praised, and I am saved from my enemies.

2 Samuel 22:2, 4

When the poor and needy seek water, and there is none, and their tongue is parched with thirst, I the Lord will answer them, I the God of Israel will not forsake them.

Isaiah 41:17

While he was in distress he entreated the favor of the Lord his God and humbled himself greatly before the God of his ancestors. He prayed to him, and God received his entreaty, heard his plea, and restored him again to Jerusalem and to his kingdom.

2 Chronicles 33:12-13

By then he was very thirsty, and he called on the Lord, saying, "You have granted this great victory by the hand of your servant. Am I now to die of thirst, and fall into the hands of the uncircumcised?" So God split open the hollow place that is at Lehi, and water came from it. When he drank, his spirit returned, and he revived.

Judges 15:18-19

REFLECTIONS

THANKSGIVING

Gratitude, appreciation, recognition,
acknowledgement, satisfaction

Rejoice always, pray without ceasing, give thanks in all circumstances; for this is the will of God in Jesus Christ for you.

1 Thessalonians 5:16-18

Blessed be the Lord, for he has heard the sound of my pleadings. The Lord is my strength and my shield; so I am helped, and my heart exults, with my song I give thanks to him.

Psalms 28:6-7

I give you thanks, O Lord, with my whole heart; I bow down toward your holy temple and give thanks to your holy name for your steadfast love and your faithfulness . . . On the day I called, you answered me, you increased my strength of soul.

Psalms 138:1-3

Open to me the gates of righteousness, that I may enter through them and give thanks to the Lord. I thank you that you have answered me and have become my salvation.

Psalms 118:19, 21

He who rescued us from so deadly a peril will continue to rescue us; on him we have set our hope that he will rescue us again, as you also join in helping us by your prayers, so that many will give thanks on our behalf for the blessings granted us through the prayers of many.

2 Corinthians 1:10-11

With joy you will draw water from the wells of salvation. And you will say in that day: Give thanks to the Lord, call on his name; make known his deeds among nations; proclaim that is name is exalted.

Isaiah 12:3-4

I will extol you, O Lord, for you have drawn me up, and did not let my foes rejoice over me. O Lord my God, I cried to you for help, and you have healed me.

Psalms 30:1-2

Blessed be the God and Father of our Lord Jesus Christ, the Father of mercies and the God of all consolation, who consoles us in all our affliction, so that we may be able to console those who are in any affliction with the consolation with which we ourselves are consoled by God.

2 Corinthians 1:3-4

In our prayers for you we always thank God the Father of our Lord Jesus Christ, for we have heard of your faith in Christ Jesus and of the love you have for the saints, because of the hope laid up for you in heaven. You have heard of this hope before in the truth, the gospel that has come to you.

Colossians 1:3-6

With gratitude in your hearts sing psalms, hymns, and spiritual songs to God. And whatever you do, in word or deed, do everything in the name of the Lord Jesus, giving thanks to God the Father through him.

Colossians 3:16-17

REFLECTIONS

UNDERSTANDING

*Knowledge, discernment, wisdom, judgment, guidance,
realization, empathy, compassion*

Therefore I prayed, and understanding was given me. I called on God, and the spirit of wisdom came to me.

Wisdom 7:7

He said to me, "Do not fear, Daniel, for from the first day that you set your mind to gain understanding and to humble yourself before your God, your words have been heard, and I have come because of your words."

Daniel 10:12

God said to him, "Because you have asked this, and have not asked for yourself long life or riches, or for the life of your enemies, but you have asked for yourself understanding to discern what is right, I now do according to your word. Indeed I give you a wise and discerning mind."

1 Kings 3:11-12

When I told of my ways, you answered me; teach me your statutes. Make me understand the way of your precepts, and I will meditate on your wondrous works.

Psalms 119:26-27

Thomas said to him. "Lord, we do not know where you are going. How can we know the way?" Jesus said to him, "I am the way, and the truth, and the life. No one comes to the Father except through me. If you know me, you will know my Father also."

John 14:5-7

Call to me, and I will answer you, and will tell you great and hidden things that you have not known.

Jeremiah 33:3

When they had prayed, the place in which they were gathered together was shaken; and they were all filled with the Holy Spirit and spoke the word of God with boldness.

Acts 4:31

May God grant me to speak with judgment, and to have thoughts worthy of what I have received; for he is the guide even of wisdom and the corrector of the wise. For both we and our words are in his hand, as are all understanding and skill in crafts. For it is he who gave me unerring knowledge of what exists, to know the structure of the world and the activity of the elements.

Wisdom 7:15, 17

"What no eye has seen, nor ear heard, nor human heart conceived, what God has prepared for those who love him" — these things God has revealed to us through the Spirit . . . Now we have received not the spirit of the world, but the Spirit that is from God, so that we may understand the gifts bestowed on us by God.

1 Corinthians 2:9-10, 12

He will surely be gracious to you at the sound of your cry; when he hears it he will answer you. And when you turn to the right or when you turn to the left, your ears shall hear a word behind you, saying, "This is the way; walk in it."

Isaiah 30:19, 21

REFLECTIONS

WORRY

Fear, doubt, anxiety, consolation, distress,
apprehension, uneasiness

Do not worry about anything, but in everything by prayer and supplication with thanksgiving let your requests be made known to God. And the peace of God, which surpasses all understanding, will guard your hearts and minds in Christ Jesus.

Philippians 4:6-7

For in everything, O Lord, you have exalted and glorified your people, and you have not neglected to help them at all times and in all places.

Wisdom 19:22

Humble yourselves therefore under the mighty hand of God, so that he may exalt you in due time. Cast all anxiety on him, because he cares for you. And after you have suffered for a while, the God of all grace, who has called you to his eternal glory in Christ, will himself restore, support, strengthen, and establish you.

1 Peter 5:6-7, 10

Therefore do not worry, saying, "What will we eat?" or "What will we drink?" or "What will we wear?" For it is Gentiles who strive for all these things; and indeed your heavenly Father knows that you need all these things. But strive first for the kingdom of God and his righteousness, and all these things will be given to you as well. So do not worry about tomorrow for tomorrow will have worries of its own. Today's trouble is enough for today.

Matthew 6:31-34

Out of my distress I called on the Lord, the Lord answered me and set me in a broad place. With the Lord on my side I do not fear. What can mortals do to me?

Psalms 11:5-6

The Lord is near to all who call on him. He fulfills the desire of all who fear him; He also hears their cry, and saves them.

Psalms 145:18-19

Keep your lives free from the love of money, and be content with what you have; for he has said, "I will never forsake you." So we can all say with confidence, "The Lord is my helper; I will not be afraid. What can anyone do to me?"

Hebrews 13:5-6

Call on me in the day of trouble; I will deliver you, and you shall glorify me.

Psalms 50:15

In my distress I called upon the Lord; to my God I cried for help. From his temple he heard my voice, and my cry to him reached his ears.

Psalms 18:6

But when he noticed the strong wind, he became frightened, and beginning to sink, he cried out, "Lord, save me!" Jesus immediately reached out his hand and caught him, saying to him, "You of little faith, why did you doubt?"

Matthew 14:30-31

REFLECTIONS

Blessings

Scripture tells us that whenever two or three are gathered in His name God will be present. Many more than two gathered together to help make God present through this book. It would be impossible to mention everyone, but a number of individuals have played a significant part on this journey. I would like to express my gratitude to:

My Family — *for their patience and understanding during the writing process; and for their faith and belief in me.*

Nora Murray, Jeanette Meyer, and Barb Moxness — *for helping me pull my thoughts together and their much-appreciated editorial assistance.*

Betty Liedtke — *for helping me convert my thoughts and ideas into a coherent text. This book would still be a work-in-progress without your expertise and professionalism.*

Sheri' Taber — *for her invaluable encouragement and support in helping me remember that God doesn't call the equipped. He equips the called.*

Mary Jo Bangasser, Pat Dolejsi, Joyce Degidio, Craig Edwards, Sue Edwards, Bill Heiman, Catherine Hering, Ray Gilgenbach, Kate Kolbe, Peter Mohs, Emily Selenski, Kim Spinner, Mike Spinner, Carol Steehler, and Ann Woessner — *for generously giving their time to search for scripture verses and review the manuscript.*

Connie Anderson, Sharon Hendry, Janice Novak, Andi Saylor, Colleen Szot, and the entire WOW group — *for their willingness to share their expertise.*

And to the many more who have offered their prayers throughout this process.

Doubt No More happened with the help and inspiration of all of you . . . each one a BLESSING to me!

Mary Jo Sherwood

is an award-winning
marketing professional,
a nationally recognized
educational and
motivational speaker,
and a contributor to the
best-selling business
book, *Masters of Success*.

Doubt No More is her first inspirational book.
Born in Milwaukee and raised in Chicago, she resides
in the Minneapolis area with her husband and their
three children.

Discounts available on this book when ordered
in quantity for bulk purchases or special sales.

For more information, please contact:

BTW Press Promotions Department
P.O. Box 554
Chanhassen, MN 55317
1.866.818.8029
promotions@btwpress.com